2/12

NATION OF
IMMIGRANTS

12 IMMIGRANTS WHO MADE
AMERICAN
MEDICINE GREAT

by Meg Marquardt

12 STORY LIBRARY

www.12StoryLibrary.com

12-Story Library is an imprint of Bookstaves.

Photographs ©: Vittoriano Rastelli/Corbis via Getty Images, cover, 1, 4; History of the Marine Biological Laboratory/CC3.0, 6; History of the Marine Biological Laboratory/CC3.0, 7; Smithsonian Institution/CC, 8; PD, 9; Keystone Pictures USA/Alamy Stock Photo, 10; Andrea Danti/Shutterstock.com, 11; PD, 12; Paul Shane/Associated Press, 13; Cliotta/CC3.0, 14; Karon Flage/CC2.0, 15; Oregon State University/CC2.0, 16; anyaivanova/Shutterstock.com, 17; Bill Branson/PD, 18; Medical Art Inc/Shutterstock.com, 19; Conrad Erb/Science History Institute/CC3.0, 20; US Department of Energy Human Genome Program/PD, 21; eLife Sciences Publications, Ltd/CC3.0, 22; ZUMA Press, Inc./Alamy Stock Photo, 23; National Institutes of Health (NIH) Image Bank/PD, 24; National Institutes of Health (NIH)/PD, 25; Damian Dovarganes/Associated Press, 26; arindambanerjee/Shutterstock.com, 27; gritsalak karalak/Shutterstock.com, 28; Keystone/PD, 29

ISBN
978-1-63235-574-4 (hardcover)
978-1-63235-628-4 (paperback)
978-1-63235-689-5 (ebook)

Library of Congress Control Number: 2018943231

Printed in the United States of America
Mankato, MN
June 2018

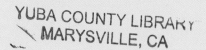
About the Cover
Rita Levi-Montalcini in 1988.

Access free, up-to-date content on this topic plus a full digital version of this book. Scan the QR code on page 31 or use your school's login at 12StoryLibrary.com.

Table of Contents

Rita Levi-Montalcini Learns How Nerves Grow

Nothing could keep Rita Levi-Montalcini from doing science. Not even World War II. She was born in Turin, Italy, on April 22, 1909. In 1936, she graduated from medical school. By that time, life in Europe was difficult for some people. Especially for Jews. The Levi-Montalcini family was Jewish.

But hardship didn't stop her. She built laboratories in her home. Even when Italy was being bombed, she kept doing research on nerve cells.

Nerves are long fibers that run through the whole body. They send signals back to the brain. These signals tell the brain if something is hot or cold, soft or hard. Nerves also sense pain.

World War II ended in 1945. After the war, Levi-Montalcini continued her research. In 1947, she was invited to work at Washington University in St. Louis, Missouri. She studied there and did nerve growth research for 30 years.

Not much was known about how nerves grow. Levi-Montalcini's

big breakthrough came when she attached a tumor to a chicken embryo. She was working with another researcher named Stanley Cohen. Together they determined that a protein from the tumor made nerves grow. They had discovered nerve growth factor (NGF).

Levi-Montalcini and Cohen won the 1986 Nobel Prize in Physiology or Medicine. Their discovery has helped doctors understand and treat diseases like Alzheimer's and cancer. In 1987, Levi-Montalcini won the National Medal of Science. This is the United States' highest scientific honor.

In 2009, Levi-Montalcini was the first Nobel laureate to reach the age of 100. She lived to be 103.

268
Miles per hour (431.3 km/h) that signals move along nerves.

- Rita Levi-Montalcini came to the United States in 1947.
- Her research led to the discovery of nerve growth factor.
- She won a Nobel Prize in 1986.

George Clowes Advances Cancer Treatment

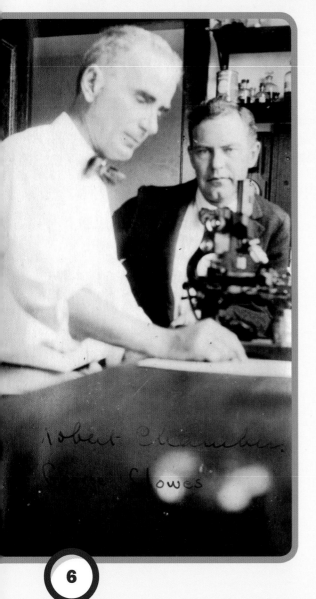

Robert Chambers
George Clowes

George Henry Alexander Clowes was born in England in 1877. He went to school in England and Germany. But his real work began after he immigrated to America. In 1901, he started work at the Institute for the Study of Malignant Diseases. These diseases can move from one part of the body to another. The most destructive one is cancer. And cancer is what Clowes wanted to defeat. In 1907, he and a group of doctors and scientists cofounded the American Association for Cancer Research (AACR).

In the early 1900s, cancer was a mystery. Doctors had known about cancer for more than 5,000 years. But they didn't know how to treat the disease. Cancer comes in hundreds of different types. Each type needs a specific treatment.

Researchers had started experimenting with chemicals to

29

Clowes's age when he cofounded the American Association for Cancer Research.

- George Clowes immigrated to the United States in 1901.
- He worked on cancer, which didn't have a good treatment.
- He developed a line of tumors that could be tested for treatments.

treat cancer. This became known as chemotherapy. However, there were many different chemicals to test. Researchers needed a better way to test treatments.

Clowes developed a transplantable line of tumors. The tumors were all identical. Being identical is important for an experiment. Scientists know that one part of the experiment will always be the same. Researchers could take Clowes's tumors and test a bunch of different drugs. Since the tumors were all alike, researchers could tell if a drug was effective. Clowes changed the way we look for treatments.

Gerty Cori Discovers How the Body Burns Energy

In the early 1900s, scientists knew that food powered the body. But they didn't know how food turned into energy. There were some clues. For instance, some people had problems with a sugar called insulin. These people came down with a disease called diabetes. So sugar had to be a piece of the puzzle.

Gerty Cori and her husband, Carl, cracked part of the code. They met in medical school in Prague, a city in what is now the Czech Republic. From then on, they were inseparable. They immigrated to the United States in 1922. They got jobs in different departments at a research center. But they kept working together. Some of their coworkers didn't like that. The Coris worked together anyway.

They uncovered an energy pathway called the Cori Cycle. It shows how energy moves from the liver into the muscles and back again. The liver stores glycogen. With oxygen, glycogen turns into glucose. Then glucose goes into muscles. It is used as someone walks or runs. The spent energy is carried back to the liver. Then the process starts all over again.

For this discovery, the Coris won the 1947 Nobel Prize in Physiology or

The Coris accepting their Nobel Prize in 1947.

Medicine. Gerty was the first woman to win this kind of Nobel Prize. She was the first American woman to win any kind of Nobel Prize.

DYNAMIC DUOS

The Coris aren't the only power couple in science. Marie and Pierre Curie won Nobel prizes for their work in physics. They discovered two radioactive elements. May Britt and Edvard Moser won by uncovering secrets in the brain. These couples prove that teamwork is sometimes best.

48

Women who have won a Nobel Prize as of 2018.

- Gerty Cori and her husband immigrated to the United States in 1922.
- Working together, they discovered how the body burns energy.
- Gerty was the first American woman to win a Nobel Prize.

Baruj Benacerraf Figures Out the Immune System

Baruj Benacerraf had a very diverse background. He was born in Venezuela in 1920, but he grew up in France. His father was Spanish and his mother was Algerian. In the 1940s, he came to the United States. He made amazing medical discoveries.

Benacerraf became known for his work with immunology. The immune system is what keeps the body healthy. When a virus or bacteria enters the body, the immune system attacks it. A strong immune system is key to a healthy life.

Before Benacerraf came along, the immune system was a puzzle. Researchers knew that white blood cells ate bacteria and viruses. But how did white blood cells know they were invaders in the first place?

With other scientists, Benacerraf found that white blood cells could read the surface of cells. Some cells have a type of molecule called an antigen. There are many different types of antigens. Certain antigens signal to the immune system that their cells are dangerous. White blood cells that come across these antigens know to attack.

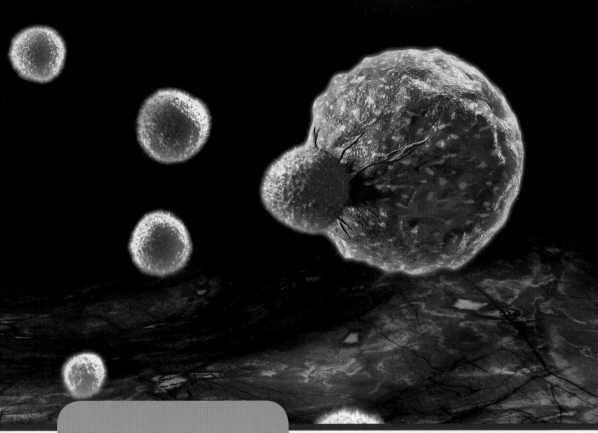

3.5–10.5 billion

Number of white blood cells in the human body.

- Benacerraf grew up in Venezuela and France.
- His work showed how the immune system works.
- He helped prove that everyone has different types of genes.

Benacerraf took this a step further. He discovered that immune response is genetic. Children inherit some of their immune system from their parents. Benacerraf helped create a theory called genetic variation. Every person has a special set of genes. No two people are exactly alike, not even identical twins.

Har Gobind Khorana Cracks the Genetic Code

molecules. These molecules are known as nucleic acids. Another set of nucleic acids takes DNA and turns it into proteins. This second set is called RNA. RNA makes the proteins that give a person brown hair and blue eyes.

However, when Khorana was doing his experiments in the 1960s, RNA was a puzzle. Scientists knew some pieces, but they didn't have a good way to test them. Khorana changed the game.

Khorana worked at the University of Wisconsin. He ran experiments there to synthesize stable DNA strands. Synthesis means putting different chemicals together to make a new chemical. In this instance, Khorana was making RNA out of nucleic acids.

Har Gobind Khorana was born in 1922. He grew up in a poor village in rural India. His father made sure his children were educated. Khorana learned to read and write. Then he went on to learn so much more.

Khorana worked with DNA. DNA is made up of only four

He was able to make the nucleic acids line up in a precise order.

420 billion

Unique DNA combinations in each generation of human beings.

- Har Khorana was born in India.
- He did research on how DNA's code turns into proteins.
- In 1986, he won a Nobel Prize.

THINK ABOUT IT

Our DNA tells us a lot about our history and our health. What is good about researchers learning more about DNA? What could possibly be bad about that?

Khorana giving a lecture at the University of Wisconsin.

This was hugely important. Because Khorana did this, researchers could try creating RNA strands that would make specific proteins. This changed the way scientists could test experiments in the lab. Khorana won the 1968 Nobel Prize in Physiology or Medicine for helping other scientists crack the genetic code.

13

Domingo Santo Liotta Invents the Artificial Heart

The first artificial heart was implanted on April 4, 1969. It was a temporary fix. A patient needed a new heart right away. But none were available. The artificial heart kept the patient alive for 64 hours. By then, there was a donor heart.

The artificial heart was created by Domingo Santo Liotta. He was an immigrant from Argentina. He did most of his schooling there. From the 1960s on, he was a top heart researcher in the United States.

Hearts fail for a lot of reasons. Sometimes it's a genetic disease. Sometimes parts of the heart get blocked. Once a heart starts to fail, it needs to be replaced. A transplant can save a person. But what happens if a transplant isn't ready?

Liotta sought to solve this problem. He wanted to keep patients alive until a transplant was ready. He created a heart-shaped pump out of plastic. It had chambers, just like a real heart. It was hooked up to arteries with tubes. Inside was a pump that moved blood through the heart and back into the body. It wasn't very sophisticated, but it was the first of its kind. It opened the door to all sorts of artificial organs.

Liotta's first artificial heart is preserved at the National Museum of American History.

ARTIFICIAL ORGANS

Hearts aren't the only artificial organs. Researchers have created artificial eyes, livers, and kidneys. Not all are ready for implants, though. Many researchers are trying to figure out how to grow real organs in labs. That way, people won't have to wait for transplants.

100,000+
Number of times a heart beats each day.

- Liotta immigrated to the United States in the 1960s.
- He designed the first artificial heart.
- The heart kept a person alive for 64 hours.

Mario Ramberg Capecchi Makes Knockout Mice

Mario Ramberg Capecchi was born in Italy at the start of World War II. After the war, he and his mother moved to the United States.

Capecchi earned a degree in biophysics. Biophysicists investigate what sort of laws biology follows. For example, they look at how different networks in the body work, such as how nerves communicate.

Capecchi's work focused on the network of genes. When he was running experiments in the 1980s, researchers understood genes had major impacts on diseases. However, there are so many different genes, it's hard to know what sort of effect a single gene might have.

Capecchi created a way to discover what a single gene does. He developed the first line of transgenic mice. Transgenic mice are also called knockout mice. That's because they have a single gene turned off, or knocked out.

Capecchi made strands of DNA in the lab. In these strands, a particular gene would be turned off. He would put these DNA strands into a mouse embryo. The embryo would develop without that gene.

Capecchi's knockout mice revolutionized biology. Today researchers all over the globe can study how specific genes function. For his work, Capecchi won a 2007 Nobel Prize for Physiology or Medicine.

ANIMAL MODELS

Mice aren't the only animals used in medical research. Another popular animal is the fruit fly. Flies are used to study gene mutations. Zebra fish are used to study organ growth. Even worms are used. Scientists study worms as a way to better understand the aging process.

30,000
Number of genes in the human genome.

- Capecchi came to the United States after World War II.
- He got a degree in biophysics.
- He created knockout mice, which helped other researchers work on genetic problems.

Flossie Wong-Staal Finds the Cause of AIDS

In 1981, a strange new illness was identified. Patients were dying of rare lung diseases and cancers. Scientists at the Centers for Disease Control and Prevention tracked the disease. In one year, almost 300 cases were reported. Over 100 people died. By September 1982, the disease had a name. It was called Acquired Immune Deficiency Syndrome (AIDS).

However, no one knew what was causing AIDS.

At this time, Flossie Wong-Staal was already hard at work as a biologist. Wang-Staal was born in China in 1952. She came to the United States in 1965 for college. In the 1970s, she started working on retroviruses at the National Cancer Institute.

Retroviruses are a specific type of infection. They invade a cell and take over its DNA. When the infected cells divide into more cells, they create more of the retrovirus's DNA. The person's own body makes more of the disease.

In 1981, when AIDS was on the rise, researchers thought it must be caused by a retrovirus. Wong-Staal identified human immunodeficiency virus (HIV) as a cause of AIDS. More importantly, she was able to identify part of what made HIV so deadly.

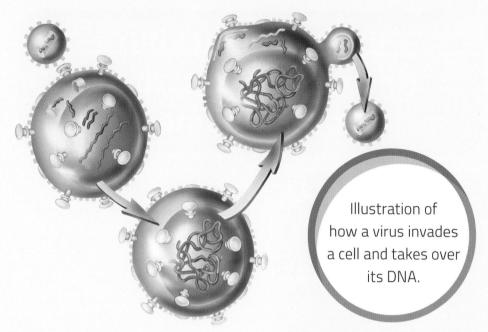

Illustration of how a virus invades a cell and takes over its DNA.

Unlike other retroviruses, HIV can go into cells that aren't actively dividing. Its presence can be silent until a cell starts dividing again. So HIV can be dormant for a long time before bursting back to life. Wong-Staal's work helped other scientists find treatments for AIDS.

36.7 million
People living with AIDS worldwide as of 2016.

- Flossie Wong-Staal moved to the United States for school.
- She did retrovirus research.
- She identified HIV as the cause of AIDS.

THINK ABOUT IT

Researchers used scientific evidence to back up their claim that AIDS was caused by a retrovirus. How can you use evidence to back up things you say are true?

Elizabeth Blackburn Uncovers Clues about Chromosomes

work as a molecular biologist. She was interested in chromosomes. Chromosomes house a person's DNA. Chromosomes are inside every cell. When a cell divides, it makes a new copy of the chromosomes. That's how each cell has an identical copy of a person's DNA.

However, sometimes that division process isn't perfect. Mistakes in copying happen. As someone gets older, chromosomes are damaged. Blackburn was interested in why this damage occurs.

Elizabeth Blackburn was born on the tiny island of Tasmania. It is just to the south of Australia. In 1948, the year she was born, only 250,000 people lived on the island. One of them would go on to win a Nobel Prize.

At the end of each chromosome is a string of DNA. The string is called a telomere. Blackburn sequenced telomeres for the first time. Sequencing means she discovered the order of a telomere's genetic code.

Blackburn moved to the United States in 1975 to

When she sequenced the telomeres, she discovered something

23

Pairs of human chromosomes.

- Elizabeth Blackburn is a molecular biologist.
- She worked to understand chromosomes.
- She discovered that telomeres protect DNA.

ANTIOXIDANTS AND TELOMERES

Aging causes two big problems. They are loss of telomeres and oxidative stress. Oxidative stress happens when certain oxygen molecules damage our DNA and telomeres. We need oxygen to survive. But oxygen also makes us age. If we could repair the damage caused by oxidative stress, we could live a lot longer. Scientists are working on this now.

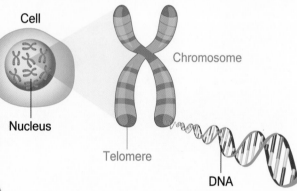

Cell

Nucleus

Chromosome

Telomere

DNA

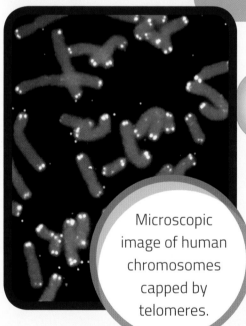

Microscopic image of human chromosomes capped by telomeres.

fascinating. Telomeres protect DNA. Each time DNA replicates, the end part of the chromosome breaks away. Since the end of the chromosome is a telomere, the actual important DNA is protected.

Blackburn's research earned her the 2009 Nobel Prize in Physiology or Medicine. She continued to work on telomeres. Her research showed that telomeres are related to both cancer and aging.

Huda Y. Zoghbi Identifies the Cause of a Rare Disease

In 1983, Dr. Huda Y. Zoghbi read an article about a new childhood syndrome. It was called Rett Syndrome. Children who suddenly develop it lose speech. They start to constantly wring their hands. It is a rare syndrome. It only affects about 1 in every 10,000 females.

After she read the article, Zoghbi met two girls with Rett Syndrome. For such a rare syndrome, she suddenly had two patients with it. Ever since, Zoghbi has dedicated her work to finding out how the syndrome works.

Zoghbi was born in Lebanon. She was in medical school when civil war broke out in 1975. She and her family ended up in the United States. Zoghbi finished medical school in Tennessee.

Though she started her career as a practicing doctor, Zoghbi soon began doing genetic research. After meeting the two girls with Rett Syndrome, she started researching what might cause it. She was the first to diagnose children with the disease in the United States. Those two girls quickly became 30 girls.

1

Percent chance that Rett Syndrome will be passed from one generation to the next.

- Zoghbi fled the civil war in Lebanon for the United States.
- She became a leading expert on a rare disease.
- Her research uncovered the cause of Rett Syndrome.

THE SHAW PRIZE

Zoghbi was awarded the Shaw Prize in 2016 for her work in the field of medicine.

MATHEMATICAL SCIENCES

LIFE SCIENCE & ME

MATHEMATICAL SCIENCES

Zoghbi went on to discover that a single gene causes Rett Syndrome. The gene is called *MECP2*. Her discovery helped researchers identify how *MECP2* causes other disorders, too. The gene is linked to other learning disorders and autism. Her work on a rare disorder has helped researchers all over the world.

Nora Volkow
Explains Drug Addiction

States to become a psychiatrist. She was interested in how drugs seem to take over a person's mind. Even though drugs cause so much damage, people keep taking even more.

She discovered that taking drugs actually changes the brain. It causes a chemical in the brain called dopamine to go wild. Dopamine makes people feel happy. So people want to take drugs again. As they take more drugs, their brains begin to change. Their outlook on the world changes, too. This makes it even harder to quit taking drugs. They don't just want drugs. They *need* them.

Volkow's work has changed the way people view addiction. It's not just about bad choices. It's also about changes in the brain. These changes may be treatable. In 2003, Volkow became director of the National Institute on Drug Abuse (NIDA). She is the first woman to hold that job.

Drug addiction hasn't always been considered a disease. For a long time, people thought it was a choice people make. Nora Volkow has led the way in proving that addiction is a disease people can't fully control.

Nora Volkow was born and raised in Mexico City. She moved to the United

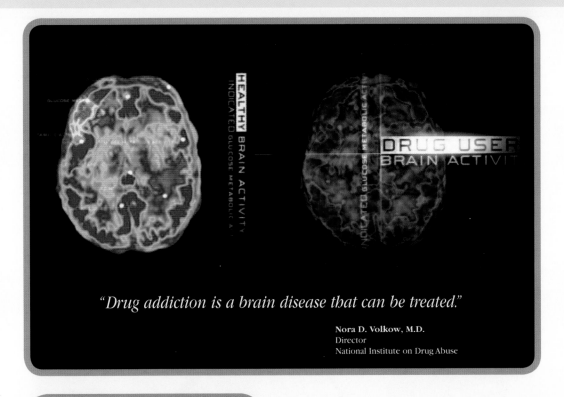

"Drug addiction is a brain disease that can be treated."

Nora D. Volkow, M.D.
Director
National Institute on Drug Abuse

$20 billion

Annual health care costs for treating illegal drug use.

- Nora Volkow was born and raised in Mexico City.
- She has pioneered understanding drug addiction as a medical problem.
- She showed how changing dopamine levels can permanently alter the brain.

THE OPIOID CRISIS

Understanding drug addiction is more important than ever. In 2017, the United States acknowledged it has an opioid crisis. Over 60,000 people died from accidental overdoses in 2016. Opioid drugs are often prescribed to treat pain. However, they are easy to get addicted to. Researchers are focusing a huge amount of energy on treatment and prevention.

Henri Ronald Ford Helps His Home Country

Henri R. Ford, MD

In 2010, a horrible earthquake struck Haiti. Over 300,000 people died. More than a million people lost their homes. Long after the disaster, people were still struggling.

Dr. Henri Ford was born in Haiti. When he was 13, his family fled the country. Haiti at the time was ruled by a dictator. Ford's family ended up in the United States. He went to medical school at Harvard University.

Ford's work focused on pediatric medicine. He's an expert on a disease called necrotizing enterocolitis. This disease affects premature babies. The bacteria that causes the disease gets into a baby's intestines. Eventually, it destroys them. Ford has worked to understand how necrotizing enterocolitis works in the body. That has led to treatments helping children around the world.

THINK ABOUT IT

Much of the world needs access to good health care. What are ways you could help others in need?

surgery, they were successfully separated.

In 2018, Ford became the new dean of the school of medicine at the University of Miami. One reason he took the job was because the University has helped the people of Haiti.

Ford never stopped thinking about his home country of Haiti. After the earthquake, he helped get medical aid to the island. He travels to Haiti several times a year. He works as a doctor and trains surgeons. He is trying to help Haiti build a sound health care system.

In 2015, Ford performed the first-ever surgery to separate conjoined twins. The twins were connected at the stomach. After a seven-hour

50
Percent of health care centers in Haiti destroyed in the 2010 earthquake.

- Henri Ford fled to the United States to escape oppression.
- He discovered the way some dangerous bacteria hurt premature babies.
- He spends time and energy giving back to Haiti.

Carl Djerassi

Djerassi was born in Austria. He fled Nazi Germany during World War II. After arriving in the United States, he studied male and female hormones. He was interested in the way fluctuations in hormones causes changes in the body. He invented the first birth control pill.

Elizabeth Stern

Originally from Canada, Stern studied pathology. Pathology is the study of how a disease progresses. She discovered over 250 different stages that a type of cancer cell goes through. This was important work. It allowed other doctors to identify a cancerous cell earlier.

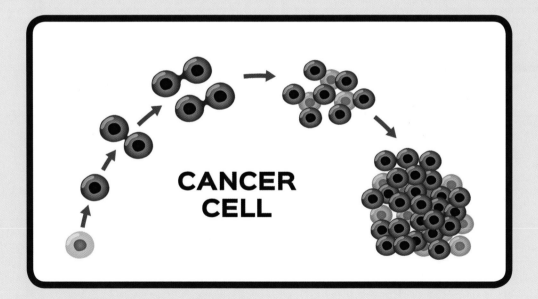

CANCER CELL

Vladimir Zworykin

Born in Russia, Zworykin was an engineer who invented all kinds of devices. He created a transmitter that someone could swallow. The transmitter could send back information, like a person's temperature. He even pioneered medical record keeping. He invented a small personal card that carried a person's medical history.

Albert Claude

Claude was born in Belgium in 1898. When he came to the United States, he pioneered work with microscopes. He showed that microscopes could be used to uncover what is happening inside a cell. A microscope could watch how changes in cell behavior meant changes in biological activity.

Editor's note:
America is a nation of immigrants. This series celebrates important contributions immigrants have made to medicine. In choosing the people to feature in this book, the author and 12-Story Library editors considered diversity of all kinds and the significance and stature of the work.

Glossary

cancer
An illness that happens when healthy cells turn into dangerous ones.

cell division
The way that cells create new cells.

chromosome
Chromosomes are the parts of a cell that carry genetic information.

diabetes
A disease where the body cannot properly process sugar.

DNA
The part of a chromosome that has genes.

embryo
An unborn human or animal at the earliest stages of growth.

genes
Biological compounds that are passed from parents to children.

genome
An organism's complete set of DNA, including all of its genes.

molecule
A small chemical compound that can take part in chemical reactions.

protein
A biological compound that creates traits like hair or eye color.

RNA
A chain of cells that processes protein.

signals
Information sent by cells to the brain.

syndrome
A disease or disorder that has many different symptoms.

transplant
Putting a new organ into the body.

tumor
An abnormal mass of new tissue growing where it shouldn't be growing.

For More Information

Books

Bendick, Jeanne. *Galen and the Gateway to Medicine.* Bathgate, ND: Bethlehem Books, 2002.

Farndon, John. *Strange Medicine: A History of Medical Remedies.* Minneapolis: Hungry Tomato, a Division of Lerner Publishing, 2017.

Elliott, Lynne. *Medieval Medicine and the Plague.* New York: Crabtree Publishing, 2006.

Visit 12StoryLibrary.com

Scan the code or use your school's login at **12StoryLibrary.com** for recent updates about this topic and a full digital version of this book. Enjoy free access to:

- Digital ebook
- Breaking news updates
- Live content feeds
- Videos, interactive maps, and graphics
- Additional web resources

Note to educators: Visit 12StoryLibrary.com/register to sign up for free premium website access. Enjoy live content plus a full digital version of every 12-Story Library book you own for every student at your school.

Index

About the Author

Meg Marquardt started out as a scientist but likes writing about science even more. She enjoys researching physics, geology, and climate science. She lives in Madison, Wisconsin with her two scientist cats, Lagrange and Doppler.